My Little Book of Happy Angels

Sue Glover and Terry Stares

Illustrations by Ian Ellis

First published in Great Britain 2019.
Pink Parties Press,
1 Ermine Street,
Ancaster,
Lincolnshire NG32 3PL.

Copyright © 2019 Sue Glover and Terry Stares.

Reformatted from Twelve Happy Angels.

Illustrations by Ian Ellis.

Pictures Digitally Remastered by Abbirose Adey (Pink Parties Press).

Photoshop work by Rose Grey.

The moral rights of the authors have been asserted.

All Rights Reserved.

British Library Cataloguing in Publication Data is available.

ISBN:978-0-995 6231-9-4

Contact: Sueglover34@btinternet.com

All net profits will be donated to:
The Alexander Devine Children's Hospice.

Dedication

We would like to dedicate this book to our Grandchildren.

We would also like to thank Ian Ellis for his subtle illustrations which brought our characters to life.

Our special thanks go to our friends and family for supporting us with this venture.

About the Authors

My Little Book of Happy Angels was an idea by Sue Glover, inspired by a lifelong love of children, animals, flowers and angels. Sue enlisted her dear friends to help with the stories, some of which started out as bedtime stories she used to make up for her grandchildren.

With the help of her close friends Terry Stares and Ian Ellis My Little Book of Happy Angels is now complete and available to be shared with families around the world. The net proceeds from sales will be donated to various children's charities.

Contents

Alice 1

Becci 5

Emily 9

Gabriella 13

Georgia 17

Holly 21

Isabella 25

Jasmine 29

Mary 33

Olive 37

Rosie 41

Sophie 45

Twelve Happy Angels

We find the Happy Angels sitting on the clouds

swaying, playing and laughing very loud.

Each one has a job to do but they'd rather have their fun,

hiding from Mr Thunder and the work that he wants done.

He asked them most politely if they would really mind,

help him clear all the bits his storm had left behind.

Coming out of hiding oh wouldn't that be fun,

helping Mr Thunder make way for Mr Sun.

Alice

It was a lovely sunny morning as Alice ran down to the meadow to play with her friends.

"Good morning Mr Toad," she said as he was hopping by.

"Goo-ood morning, please call me Toady, all my other friends do." said Mr Toad gruffly.

"Oh dear, what is wrong with your croak today?" asked Alice, "You always have such a loud clear croak."

"I have rather a sore throat," he said.

"I'd better see what I can do," said Alice.

Suddenly, she noticed her friend Elsie the earthworm curled up under a log.

"Can you help Mr Toad?" she asked.

"Oh no I'm too tired and I need to keep cool as it looks like it's going to be a very hot day," replied Elsie.

"Okay," said Alice.

She then spotted the giggling butterfies who were always very silly, flying around.

"Please can you help Mr Toad?" Alice asked.

"Oh no," they all cried out, "we have to flitter and flap our wings so we can keep cool."

"Alright," said Alice as she sat on the big log.

Suddenly, Mrs Ladybird landed near her.

"Please can you help Mr Toad with his very croaky voice?" Alice asked.

"Oh no dear, not today," she said as she gave a big yawn. Then she quickly fell asleep on Alice's sleeve.

Suddenly, Alice heard zzzzzzzzz…zzzzzzzzzz

"Oh Mr Bumber," Alice cried out. Her friend the bumblebee had just come into view. "Please could you help Mr Toad with his very croaky voice?" Alice begged, smiling sweetly.

"I'm getting fed up with everyone wanting my help when they have a sore throat," said Mr Bumber. "Mmmm," he thought for a minute and told Alice to tell Toady to wait for him by the large log and he would come and visit him.

It wasn't long before Mr Bumber kept his word and brought Toady a large spoon of fresh honey.

"Mmmm, that was lovely," cried Toady. "My throat is feeling so much better now, thank you Alice."

"Don't thank me, thank Mr Bumber," Alice said.

'Well, I had better get home,' she thought.

Alice was so pleased to see her friends and help Toady as well.

"Bye all," she shouted, "see you tomorrow."

They all waved as Alice left the meadow.

Poem for Alice

Alice loves the butterflies and their coloured wings.

She's friendly with the bumblebees and creepy crawly things.

She's fond of Mrs Ladybird with spots upon her back,

And wonders why she always wears her coat of red and black.

Becci

Whenever Friday came around, the wonderful smells of baking came from Becci's kitchen. The Happy Angels wondered what Becci was making today.

They watched through the open kitchen window as she mixed the sugar, the butter, the flour and the eggs together.

She put the cake mixture into her favourite bowl, which she placed on the kitchen windowsill. Everyone knew Becci made the most fabulous cakes.

Her curious little friends were so eager to taste the cake mixture and in their excitement they tugged and pulled the

bowl so hard that it went flying off the windowsill…

… SPLAT!

The whole mixture landed on the floor. Just then, Becci walked in and saw what had happened.

"Oh dear, what have you done?" she exclaimed, "I'll have to start all over again. So don't expect any cakes for tea today."

They hung their heads down low and felt very sorry for being so silly.

After a while, they could smell the wonderful cakes cooking.

"Oh, there are none for us today," they cried, "It was our fault anyway."

Becci came out from the kitchen with plates of sticky buns, fairy cakes, chocolate cakes and lots and lots of biscuits.

The Happy Angels were peeping out from behind the bushes and were watching hungrily as all the wonderful cakes were laid out on the table for tea.

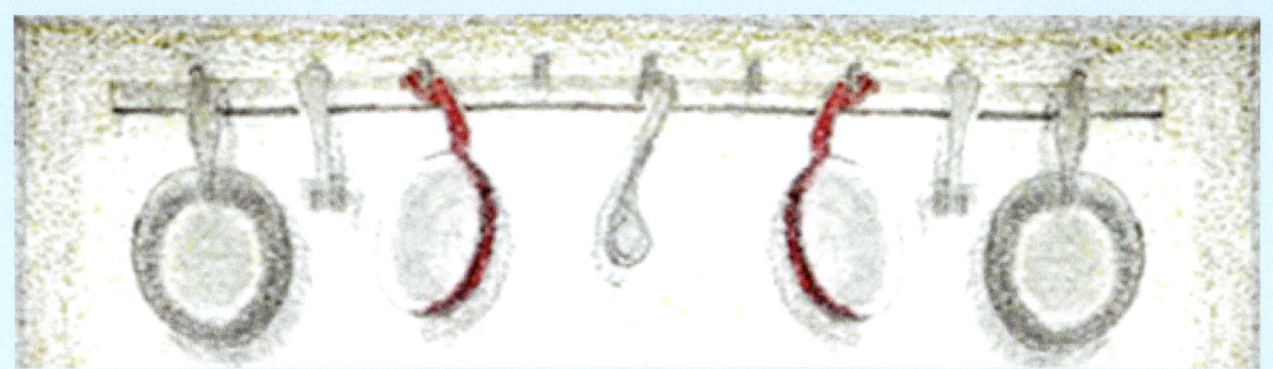

From the shelter of the bushes they whispered,

"Sorry Becci, sorry."

Becci turned round and smiled. "Come on out," she said, "I have made them all for you anyway."

You have never seen such happy angels. You would think from the look on their faces that they had never had cake before!

Poem for Becci

Becci Biscuit bakes all day and finds it all such fun.

She makes cherry pies, fairy cakes and lots of sticky buns.

The smell of baking fills the air and you should see them smile,

When all the cakes are handed out it drives the angels wild.

Emily

Emily wasn't really tired but was so used to daydreaming. She found a quiet spot, closed her eyes and waited to see where her daydreams would take her. Soon, she found herself sitting on a big, white, fluffy cloud drifting over the treetops.

'I can see everything from here,' she thought. 'Oh! There's Betty the Bluebird with her nest of eight babies, how cosy they look cuddling up to their mummy wrapped tightly in their bed sheet.'

As the cloud moved on, she saw a horse pulling a hay cart. She looked down at the fields below and noticed a field full of sheep and baby lambs. 'I wonder how many there are?' she thought as she started to count them. Feeling sleepy, Emily didn't notice the gust of wind making the cloud go faster and taking her further and further up.

Emily suddenly woke with a start and realised she was going in the wrong direction.

'What am I going to do?' she thought, 'How will I ever get home?' Emily started to worry but she was not the only one worrying. Betty the Bluebird became concerned,

"Where is Emily?" she asked her little chicks.

"We don't know!" they cried. Then one of them pointed to the sky, "There! There she is riding on a big, white cloud!"

Betty quickly flew towards Emily but the cloud was much too high.

"Help!" cried Emily.

"You must jump!" said Betty.

"But I can't, my wings are not strong enough!" Emily shouted back.

"Don't worry the little chicks will bring their bed sheet, two on each corner will be strong enough to break your fall. Harry the Horse will make sure you land safely on his hay cart," Betty said.

Emily jumped and felt herself falling like a feather. She landed with a slight bump on the hay cart, wrapped in the bluebirds' bed sheet. She then slowly slid to the ground.

"What a dream that was!" she said scratching her head. She then removed the hay from her hair and undid the bed sheet, which was wrapped tightly round her. She looked up and saw Betty the Bluebird smiling, her wings cuddling her little chicks.

Emily realised it wasn't a dream after all.

Poem for Emily

Sleepy Emily closed her eyes and had such a lovely dream,

Flying with bluebirds in the sky how lovely it all seemed.

As she drifted further she took a little doze.

She was woken by a butterfly that kissed her on her nose.

Gabriella

It was raining hard. All the Happy Angels were sheltering under the large oak tree waiting for the rain to stop. Everyone that is, except Gabriella. She just loved water, especially the rain.

She ran out from under the cover of the tree and jumped into the first big puddle she came to and splashed water all over the place.

"Excuse me," a loud voice exclaimed, "Do you mind, you are jumping in my puddle," said Dolly the Duck. "This is my training puddle for all the baby ducklings, so they can learn how to swim properly. This is not a good example you are showing them, splashing water everywhere."

"Oh! I'm very sorry," said Gabriella. She loved the ducklings and didn't want to upset them or Dolly.

She looked for a larger puddle away from the ducklings and spotted one by the bushes. As she ran to the bushes she saw naughty Foxy Fox hiding at the edge of an even bigger puddle.

He was hiding so no one could see him watching the two little ducklings who had strayed from Dolly's swimming group. The two little ducklings were so busy playing 'duck and bob' they hadn't noticed they were being watched. Foxy was looking forward to catching one of them for his tea.

'I think he's up to no good,' thought Gabriella. Quick as a flash she ran and took the biggest leap so that she made a huge splash. The water not only frightened the little ducklings back to the swimming group, but caught Foxy Fox off guard when the water went all over him. He got absolutely soaked. He ran away so fast leaving Gabriella quite surprised.

Dolly the Duck rushed up to Gabriella, put her wings around her and gave her a kiss.

"Thank you for saving my ducklings!" she said. "By the way, I've changed my mind dear. You are now welcome to join us, as I have now made you a member of the duckling's swimming group and you can come and splash as much as you like."

Gabriella was so happy to be part of Dolly Duckling's Family.

Poem for Gabriella

Gabriella Water Lily such a pretty name.

She so enjoys getting wet and playing in the rain,

And spends her time collecting all the dewdrops as they fall.

Just before she goes to bed she sits and counts them all.

Georgia

Georgia loved dancing. Every minute of every day she would dance, dance, dance. The Happy Angels loved to watch her and Georgia was delighted to dance for them.

One day, she noticed one of the Happy Angels playing with a spinning top.

'I'd like to spin like that,' thought Georgia, 'maybe I shall try and do a twirl today.'

Georgia started twirling round and round, round and round, but she didn't realise that all the twirling would make her dizzy. When she stopped, she fell over.

"Oh no!" she cried, "I've hurt my leg. I'll never be able to dance properly again!"

She began to feel sad. All the Happy Angels also felt sad.

"We must try and help her, but what can we do?" they said, "We must think of something to make her smile."

Meanwhile Georgia took to her bed, leaving the other angels deep in thought. After a while, Rosie said,

"I know, why don't we all put on our ballet shoes and dance for Georgia?"

"Yes! Yes!" the other angels cried out, "She knows we can't dance like her, and it may make her feel happy again."

With great excitement they began to dance together. They made so many mistakes, bumping into each other and dancing so badly, they kept falling over. Georgia couldn't bear to watch anymore and started laughing.

"I know," she said "I could teach you all to dance."

"But your leg?" the angels cried out.

"Wait a minute!" exclaimed Georgia.

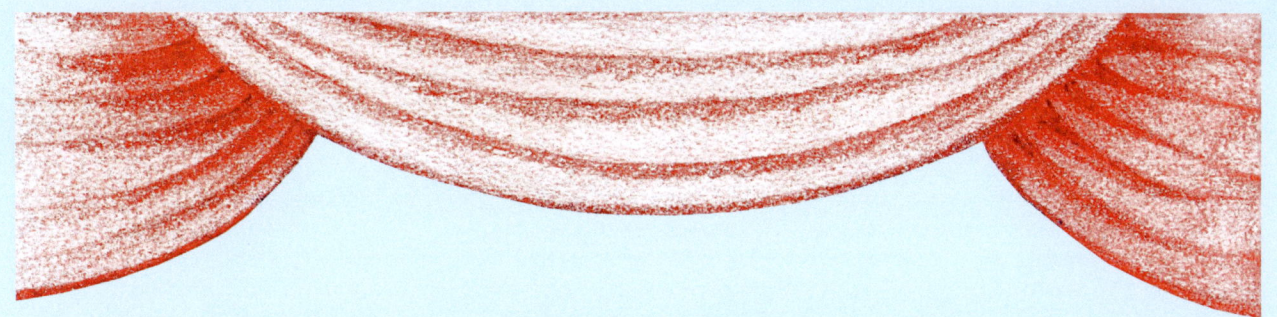

Georgia wiggled her toes then she climbed out of bed and stood up tall, pointed a toe, and started to smile.

"My leg is feeling much better and now I'm going to teach you the basic steps so we can dance together."

The Happy Angels were excited and started giggling.

"Wow, just think one day we might be as good as Georgia!

Three cheers, we couldn't have a better teacher."

Poem for Georgia

Georgia Hippy Tippy Toes loves to take a chance.

With a twinkle in her eye she'll teach you how to dance.

First a twirl, then a bow, she smiles sweetly for her friends.

She'll do her dance so gracefully, then curtsy at the end.

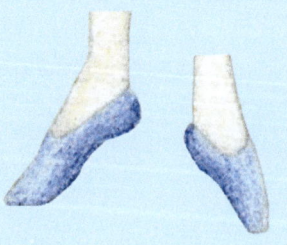

Holly

Of all the angels, Holly is quite the loudest and noisiest, especially when she gets excited. The other angels have to cover their ears when Holly calls for them as she tends to raise her voice quite loudly, she is a bit of a tomboy you see.

Holly is always climbing on anything she finds, it could be a ladder, it could be a tree or a rainbow, nothing seems to worry her, whatever it is, you can bet Holly will climb it.

"What are you going to do today?" the Happy Angels asked as they skipped behind her.

"I'm going to find the tallest tree in the wood then I am going to climb it," Holly answered.

"You mustn't go too high or you may never get down," they said.

"Oh don't worry about me," said Holly, "I'll be okay," and off she went.

Holly indeed found the largest tree and began to climb. She got higher and higher and so enjoyed her climb that she lost all track of time. Eventually, she realised she was so high up that her friends the Happy Angels looked like little dots on the ground.

'Oh dear!' thought Holly, 'I've gone too far this time, how am I going to get down, it is starting to get dark.'

Just then Olga Owl flew by.

"What is going on? Is that you Holly, disturbing me again? Just when I'm ready to look for my food."

"I'm sorry," said Holly, "I've climbed too high this time and I can't get down. Oh please help me Olga."

"I'm sorry I can't," Olga said, "as I have a bad back. I'll call on one of my friends and see if they can help." So Olga called up to her friend. "Could you please help Holly? She has been up to her tricks again and climbed much too high this time."

"Not again," grumbled Old Bertie the grand old buzzard. He flew down through the branches and told Holly to climb on his back. With a swoop he took her down to safety.

"There you are. You may not be so lucky next time. Stay on the ground and leave the trees for the birds." He muttered under his breath as he flew back up to the top of the tree.

"Thank you," said Holly, "until the next time."

"No next time," shouted Olga.

"No next time," shouted Bertie.

The Happy Angels were so pleased Holly was safe they ran up and gave her a cuddle.

"No next time," shouted the Happy Angels.

Poem for Holly

Little Holly Howler is happy as can be.

When she knows she gets the chance to climb the tallest tree.

She isn't very tidy, she isn't very shy,

And even climbs on rainbows that are hanging in the sky.

Isabella

As the Happy Angels were walking to their village they noticed a sign pinned on to a tree, 'Competition Today', it read, 'For whoever paints the prettiest picture in the village will get to paint the rainbow in the sky for all to see.'

The Happy Angels were very excited, so straight away they set about getting their paper, paints and brushes as they all wanted to paint the prettiest picture. Two happy angels painted flowers, three painted dogs and cats, two painted a village green, one painted the church with its very high steeple, and three painted each other.

Isabella wandered to the corner of the field away from the other angels and started to paint. She wanted to see how pretty she could make the rainbow look, so she gathered her paints and drew a rainbow. She decided to make the picture quite large and started to call out all the colours she was painting by singing the famous rainbow song.

Just as she had finished her painting, a gust of wind blew her painting up into a nearby tree. Isabella tried to get it down, she tried to climb the branch, then she tried using a long stick but she just could not reach.

"Where has it gone?" She looked and looked but couldn't see her painting. "Oh dear!" she said. "I won't get the chance to paint the rainbow now!"

Then the judges arrived to see all the paintings,

"How clever you all are," they said. "And where is yours?" they asked Isabella.

"The wind blew it into the trees!" she said, "I tried to get it down but I couldn't."

The judges stared at Isabella. Just then, another gust of wind blew the branches and Isabella's painting fell to the ground.

When they saw her painting, they all agreed it was the loveliest one they had seen.

"How beautiful!" they said, "It has all the correct colours. We declare you the winner and we would be delighted if you would paint the rainbow in the sky."

"Oh, thank you!" cried Isabella, her wish had now come true.

Poem for Isabella

Isabella's rainbows whose colours fill the sky,

Starting on the ground and climbing oh so high.

A staircase built of colours painted just for you,

Red and yellow, pink and green, violet, orange and blue.

Jasmine

There is never a dull moment when Jasmine is around. She likes jumping high, she likes jumping low, she never walks but always skips and runs.

One Saturday morning on Jasmine's birthday, when she had gone for her skip and jump in the woods, Holly, one of the Happy Angels came rushing in to see her friends.

"The circus is here, the circus has come to town!" They all jumped up and down clapping their hands with joy.

"There'll be lots of balloons and ice cream and funny clowns, we should all go as an extra treat for Jasmine. We'll ask Popo the clown if he will do the honours and present Jasmine with her birthday cake," said Emily. "It must be a surprise for her so we won't say anything until it's time for us to go."

"Sshh, Sshh!" they giggled.

Quietly, all the Happy Angels sat down to a scrumptious tea. Jasmine felt a little let down,

'After all, it's my birthday, and they haven't even got me a birthday cake,' she thought, 'I would have loved a birthday cake. My birthday is only once a year.'

The Happy Angels gathered together and said,

"Why don't we all go for a walk to the village. Come on Jasmine!" So off they went. They came to a field and heard all the lovely sounds of music playing and then they saw a huge red and blue tent with jugglers and clowns.

"Surprise, surprise!" the Happy Angels shouted out to Jasmine. Jasmine couldn't believe her eyes,

"Oh my gosh!" she cried, "What a lovely surprise!"

Her whole evening was made complete when the funniest clown called Popo presented her with a very large birthday cake. After the Happy Angels had sung Happy Birthday and Jasmine had blown out the candles, she said,

"I thought you had all forgotten my birthday."

"Would we ever?" the Happy Angels cried out. "We have a huge pile of presents for you at home!"

Just before they left, Popo the clown took his hat off, produced a bunch of flowers from behind his back and handed them to Jasmine, "Happy Birthday," he said with a smile.

Jasmine was so excited she hopped and skipped all the way home.

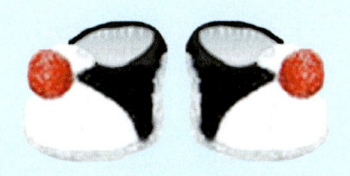

Poem for Jasmine

Jasmine's such a jumping bean who loves acting like a clown.

She seems so very happy as she keeps jumping up and down,

And always tries to do her best by jumping oh so high,

And even frightened Mr Sun as he was passing by.

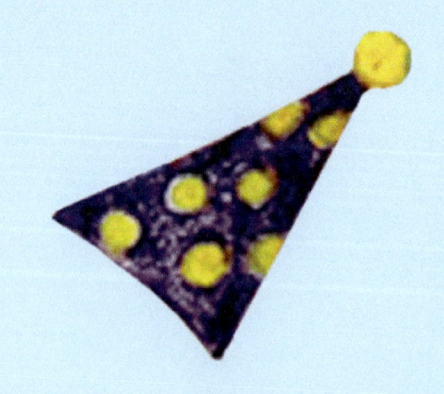

Mary

It was a gentle, autumn morning, when Mary decided to go and visit Hazel the Hedgehog, who was one of her newest friends. Mary knew where Hazel could normally be found. It was only a little way further and Mary began to hum a pretty tune as she skipped along the path between some trees. Mary called out to Hazel,

"Where are you my little friend?" There was no answer. 'Funny,' Mary thought as Hazel was always there.

Mary started to search down by the pond, then in the hedgerows in case Hazel had got caught in the brambles. She called out again but Hazel was nowhere to be seen.

Mary asked several passing birds and small creatures if any of them had seen Hazel,

"No," they all answered.

She then asked the Happy Angels if any of them had seen Hazel,

"No," they replied, "but we'll help you to look for her."

It was a great adventure for the Happy Angels, helping Mary look for Hazel. They ran all over the field, and through the trees, rolling on the grass, while calling out her name. Helping Mary was turning out to be great fun, but after a while Mary started to get very worried as they were running out of places to look.

Suddenly, there was a slight rustle from the big pile of leaves that were sitting on the ground at the foot of a large oak tree. There, Mary saw the prettiest, pink hedgehog nose. Deep from under the leaves, Hazel appeared and shouted out to Mary,

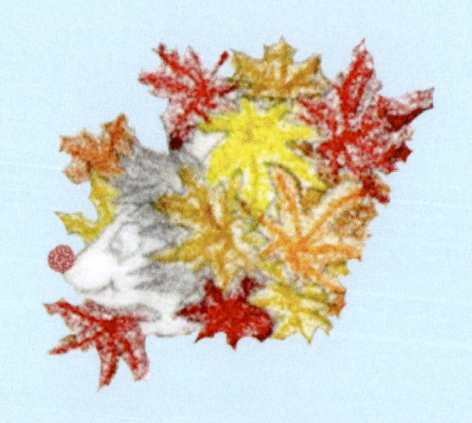

"You did give me such a shock, what is all this noise and fuss?"

"We were worried about you," said Mary.

"But I'm only practising my hibernation routine," Hazel laughed. "You see, every year I curl up in a warm pile of leaves and sleep through the winter."

"Oh! I feel so silly and I'm sorry to have disturbed you," Mary laughed.

The others joined in and so the whole woodland echoed with their laughter.

Poem for Mary

Pretty Mary loves Autumn and the falling leaves.

She tries to catch them in the air as they tumble from the trees.

All the lovely colours of orange, gold and red.

She has such fun collecting them to make a blanket for her bed.

Olive

Olive was the smallest Happy Angel, the others used to carry her around like a doll, which she liked very much. Olive had a very pretty voice and used to sing all day to herself.

One day, there was a little songbird who didn't know how to sing properly and all the other little birds used to laugh at her. They told her that her job was to sing every morning, she needed to wake up all the people so they could have their breakfast and go to work. The little songbird was sad as she wasn't doing her job very well.

From the next door garden, the little songbird heard a lovely voice. She wanted to know who was singing so beautifully, so she flew up to a branch on the tree and peeped through the leaves.

She saw a happy angel singing away to herself. The little bird smiled sweetly at the lovely sound then hung her head down low. Olive saw her and said,

"Hello, and what is your name?"

"They call me Bella," said the little bird. Olive noticed Bella looked very sad.

"Why are you so sad?" she said to the bird.

Bella explained that it was her job to sing sweetly with the other songbirds in the morning to wake everyone up, but she couldn't sing.

"Don't worry," said Olive, "Would you like me to teach you? We could sing together and that way you can learn from me."

"Oh yes please," said Bella. The very next morning, Olive and Bella went to a quiet part of the wood to practice. After a couple of days, and a lot of singing, Olive said to the songbird,

"Now you are ready to sing with the other birds as you have such a beautiful voice."

The next morning, an amazing thing happened. Bella sang so sweetly that one by one all the other birds stopped singing just to listen to Bella's beautiful voice.

Olive was so pleased as she watched Bella fly away singing loudly for everyone to hear.

Poem for Olive

Little Olive Angel whose voice you could hear for miles.

Her pretty tunes bring pleasure and oh so many smiles.

She even teaches little birds to sing their morning song,

And wake up all those sleepy heads to help each day along.

Rosie

There was an old lady with the most beautiful garden. There were so many flowers of different colours and sizes. The old lady could not stoop down to pick flowers for herself, she was too old now. She would just look at them from her window.

'How I would love to have flowers in my house,' she thought as she was gazing at her garden.

Suddenly she saw a beautiful happy angel who was skipping among the flowers. Rosie was so happy that she didn't notice the old lady watching her as she picked bunches of flowers in all colours.

She gathered reds, blues, yellows, purples, pinks and whites then sat down and started making a garland for her hair.

As she sat dreaming, she thought of the old lady who lived in the cottage and wondered how she was. It was such a long time ago that Rosie had last seen her. Suddenly, she sat up.

"Oh dear," she said to herself, "I have picked so many flowers from this lovely garden." She turned and looked towards the house and saw the shadow of the old lady watching her. Rosie waved her hand and the old lady waved back. '

I know,' she thought, 'I will take some of the flowers that I have picked and make a lovely garland for the old lady to wear.'

Rosie walked up to the house her arms filled with the most beautiful flowers.

"I've picked flowers for your house and made a garland for you to wear," said Rosie. There were tears in the old lady's eyes.

"Oh how beautiful they are!" she cried as Rosie put all the bunches of flowers in her arms, and the garland around her hair.

"You look lovely," said Rosie.

"Thank you my dear," said the old lady. "Please come again and pick as many flowers as you want from my garden."

"That's so kind," said Rosie, "I can't wait, thank you."

She turned and waved goodbye to the old lady and skipped along the path all the way home.

Poem for Rosie

Rosie Posie always knows what she likes to wear,

And picks the lovely colours of flowers for her hair.

She's always making garlands with sweet peas of red and blue,

And skips among the daisies and other flowers too.

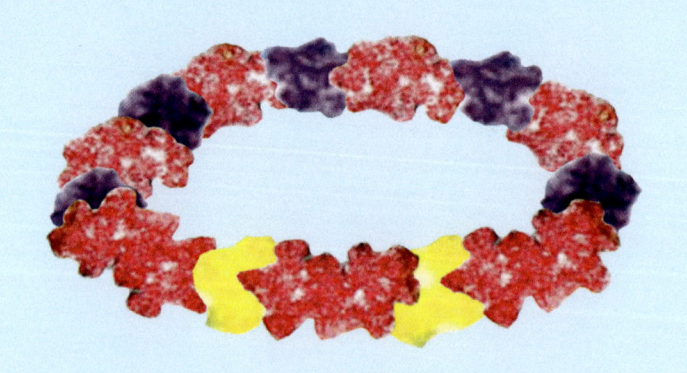

Sophie

"What are we going to do about Sophie?" the Happy Angels said. "Whenever we ask her to help with the cooking, or making the beds, or cleaning the dishes, she always says, 'In a minute,' or 'I'm busy.'"

Before you can say, 'housework', Sophie is outside climbing on a large cloud to make herself comfortable so she can laze away in the sun.

"It's not fair!" the Happy Angels cried out. "We have to do all the work while Sophie does nothing. How can we make her do her share of work?" they asked one another. They all shook their heads.

Just then Reggie Rooster walked by,

"Well what's up, what is going on?" he said.

"We don't know what to do about Sophie. We do all the work including Sophie's. It isn't fair!" they replied.

"My dears you have to have a plan. Now, what is it that Sophie loves the most?"

"She loves lazing in the sunshine doing nothing." The Happy Angels all replied together.

"Well, we'll see about that!" said Reggie.

The next day, Sophie went sunbathing on her favourite cloud instead of working. Reggie Rooster saw all this and asked Mr Sun to help out and disappear for a few hours so Mr Thunder could take his place.

Mr Thunder was happy to oblige as this was the first time someone had asked him for a thunderstorm. When he saw Sophie on her cloud he knew what he had to do. He shook the clouds about.

"What is happening?" called out Sophie. Mr Thunder started to stamp his feet and there was a terrible noise. He clapped his hands and brought out flashes of lightning. Then, he opened a very large water bag and out came the rain. Sophie, who was still on her cloud got very wet.

"Help me! help me to get down from here I will do all my jobs and help you with yours," Sophie promised.

Slowly, Mr Thunder brought the cloud lower so the Happy Angels could help Sophie into their dry, warm home. The Happy Angels winked at Mr Thunder as they waved goodbye to him.

Mr Sun peeped out from the corner of the sky, shook his head and smiled.

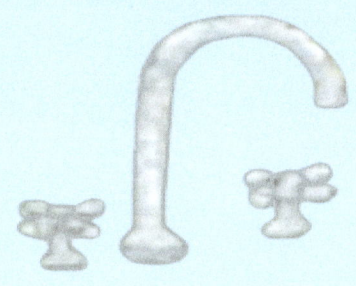

Poem for Sophie

Sophie likes to spend all day lazing in the sun,

And so enjoys relaxing when all her jobs are done.

Mr Sun tries very hard to chase the rain away,

He does his best for Sophie and tries to shine all day.

Twelve Happy Angels

For the Happy Angels it's been a busy day,
Doing all their little jobs still finding time to play.

They polished all those lovely stars to twinkle in the night,
And Mrs Moon was very pleased to see them shining bright.

These cherubs of the night sky take turns the whole night through,
Keeping all the children safe and watching over you.